COLORING
for Grown-Ups
COLLEGE COMPANION

A PLUME BOOK

COLORING
for Grown-Ups
COLLEGE COMPANION

Ryan Hunter & Taige Jensen
authors of COLORING FOR GROWN-UPS

PLUME
Published by the Penguin Group
Penguin Group (USA) LLC
375 Hudson Street
New York, New York 10014

USA | Canada | UK | Ireland | Australia | New Zealand | India | South Africa | China
penguin.com
A Penguin Random House Company

First published by Plume, a member of Penguin Group (USA) LLC, 2014

 REGISTERED TRADEMARK—MARCA REGISTRADA

ISBN 978-0-14-218141-6

Printed in the United States of America
10 9 8 7 6 5 4 3 2

Coloring for Grown-Ups
COLLEGE COMPANION
MATERIALS NEEDED:

☐ **Coloring utensils**   ☐ **Scissors**

OPTIONAL:

☐ **Social skills**   ☐ **Foamy keg beer**

☐ **Unfortunate facial hair**   ☐ **Shower shoes**

☐ **Doomed long-distance relationship**   ☐ **Desire to learn things**

GIVE YOUR DORM ROOM PERSONALITY!

Make a bold statement using the decorations on the left, or draw your own!

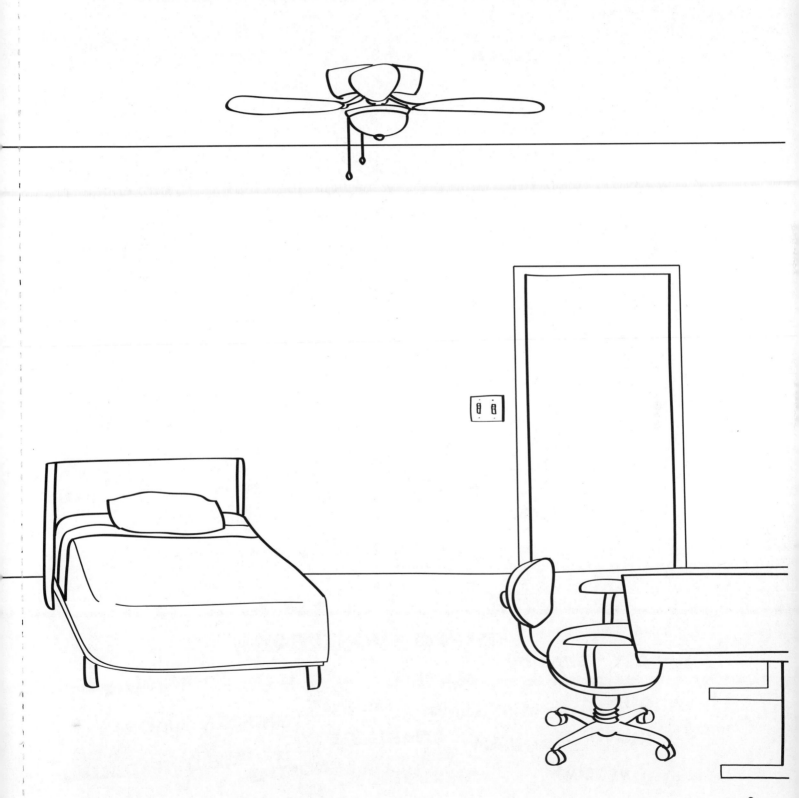

BREAK THE ICE!

Help this freshman orientation group get to know one another by giving each one a fun and memorable nickname!
REMEMBER: Alliteration is the ultimate social lubricant!

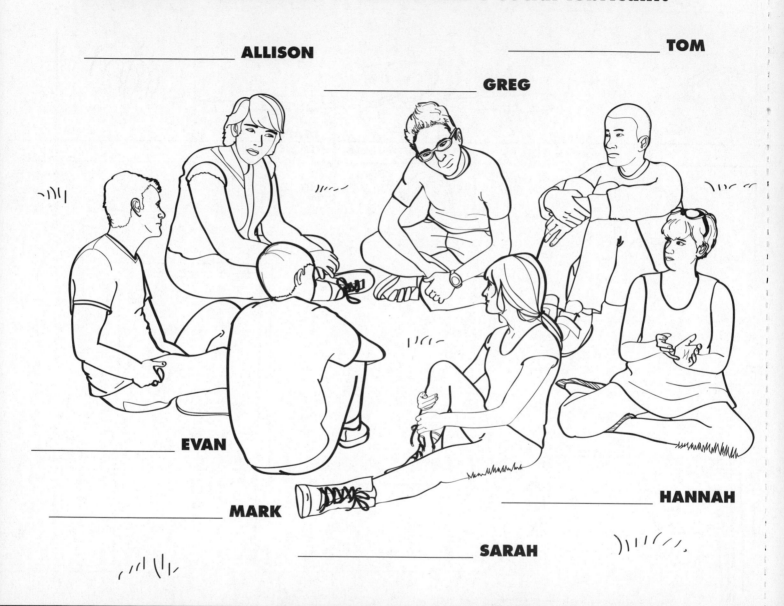

_____ ALLISON

_____ TOM

_____ GREG

_____ EVAN

_____ MARK

_____ HANNAH

_____ SARAH

HELPFUL SUGGESTIONS:

GREASY   SEASICK   TANGIBLE   THIRSTY   GLANDULAR

TROUBLED   MISSHAPEN   SUPINE   ETHNIC   AMORAL

EROTIC   HUMAN   ATTAINABLE

ADULTEROUS   GERIATRIC   HOSTILE   SESQUIPEDALIAN

QUAD

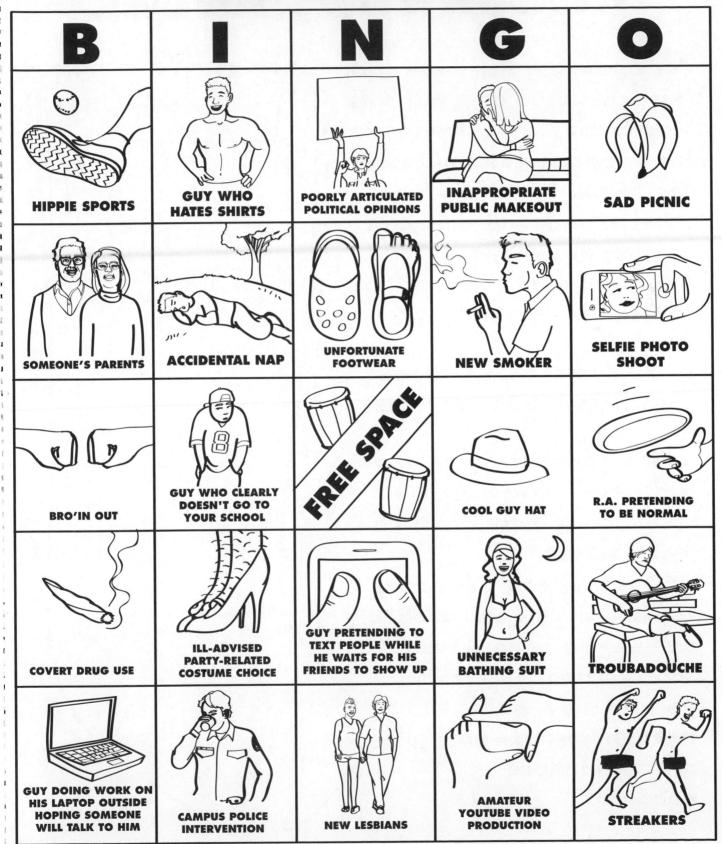

B I N G O

B	I	N	G	O
HIPPIE SPORTS	GUY WHO HATES SHIRTS	POORLY ARTICULATED POLITICAL OPINIONS	INAPPROPRIATE PUBLIC MAKEOUT	SAD PICNIC
SOMEONE'S PARENTS	ACCIDENTAL NAP	UNFORTUNATE FOOTWEAR	NEW SMOKER	SELFIE PHOTO SHOOT
BRO'IN OUT	GUY WHO CLEARLY DOESN'T GO TO YOUR SCHOOL	FREE SPACE	COOL GUY HAT	R.A. PRETENDING TO BE NORMAL
COVERT DRUG USE	ILL-ADVISED PARTY-RELATED COSTUME CHOICE	GUY PRETENDING TO TEXT PEOPLE WHILE HE WAITS FOR HIS FRIENDS TO SHOW UP	UNNECESSARY BATHING SUIT	TROUBADOUCHE
GUY DOING WORK ON HIS LAPTOP OUTSIDE HOPING SOMEONE WILL TALK TO HIM	CAMPUS POLICE INTERVENTION	NEW LESBIANS	AMATEUR YOUTUBE VIDEO PRODUCTION	STREAKERS

5

MAKESHIFT DORM SOCK DOORKNOB HANGER

For centuries, the dorm sock has been used as a fail-safe way to alert a roommate to his or her unwelcomeness in the home. Use this paper version on laundry day, or to provide additional information to your roommate and/or hall.

Examples of helpful dorm sock memos might include:

• "My underage high school girlfriend is here for the weekend (please don't be weird about it)."
• "Don't worry, I'm pretty terrible at this and probably will not be in here long."
• "I'm actually watching porn in here without headphones on—no congratulations needed!"

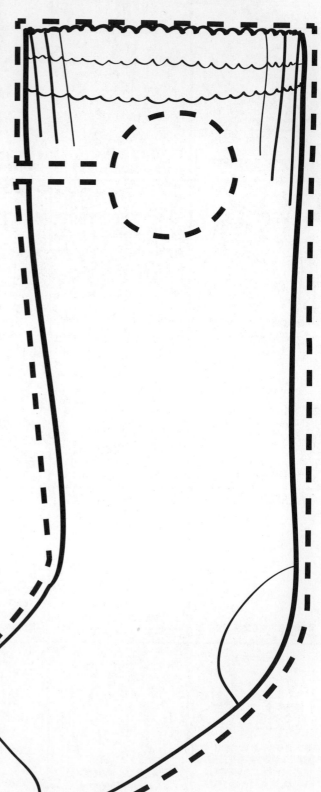

FUN ACTIVITIES

FOR PASSING THE TIME WHILE YOUR ROOMMATE HAS SEX IN YOUR ROOM

1. DESIGN YOUR OWN FAKE ID!

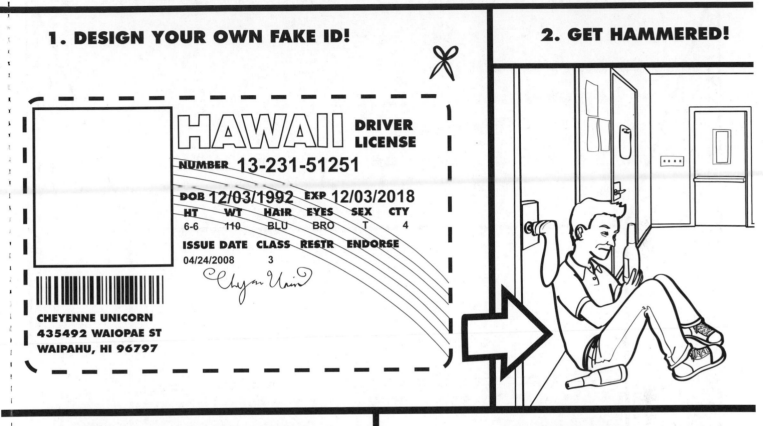

HAWAII DRIVER LICENSE

NUMBER 13-231-51251

DOB 12/03/1992   EXP 12/03/2018

HT	WT	HAIR	EYES	SEX	CTY
6-6	110	BLU	BRO	T	4

ISSUE DATE   CLASS   RESTR   ENDORSE
04/24/2008   3

CHEYENNE UNICORN
435492 WAIOPAE ST
WAIPAHU, HI 96797

2. GET HAMMERED!

3. DRAW WHAT YOU IMAGINE TO BE YOUR ROOMMATE'S FAVORITE SEXUAL POSITION!

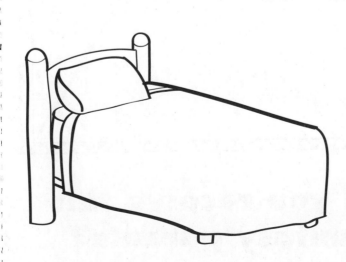

4. SUDOKU?

2				5	8		6	
	7		8	4	1			3
9	3	8					1	5
7	8		5			3		4
	1	2	4		6			
	5			9		2	8	
	2			5	4			8
	6		1	7			4	2
5	9			2		3		

DESIGN YOUR FANTASY CARE PACKAGE!

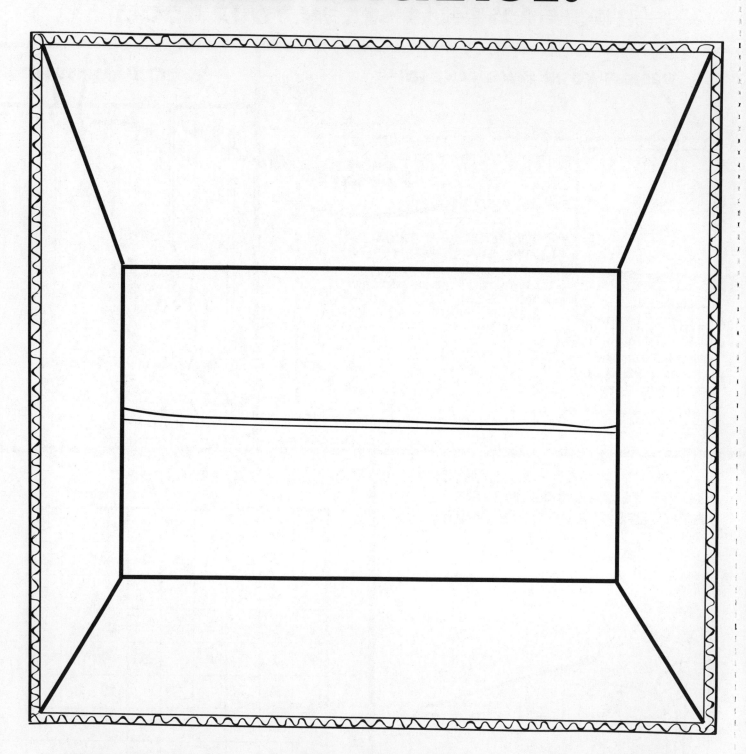

What cool stuff did you receive this week from your fantasy parents?

ROOMMATE TRIBUTE

My Roommate

Creep out your roommate by drawing his or her likeness above and "accidentally" leaving this in the common area.

REINVENT YOURSELF!

Draw the brand-new you below by adopting one or more convincing new affectations!

WHAT WILL YOU PRETEND TO BE THIS YEAR?

☐ EDGY?

☐ CHILL?

☐ "URBAN"?

☐ INTELLECTUAL?

☐ BRITISH?

☐ BROKE?

☐ ASIAN?

☐ AN IDIOT?

THE POSSIBILITIES ARE ENDLESS!

COLORFUL LANGUAGE

Your parents aren't around anymore, so you can talk however you want! Use your favorite colors to fill in each speech bubble with your favorite naughty words. Now THAT'S colorful language!

HAZE MAZE

It's rush week! Can you escape this fraternity house without receiving lasting psychological damage from your new bros?

ENTER →

ESCAPE

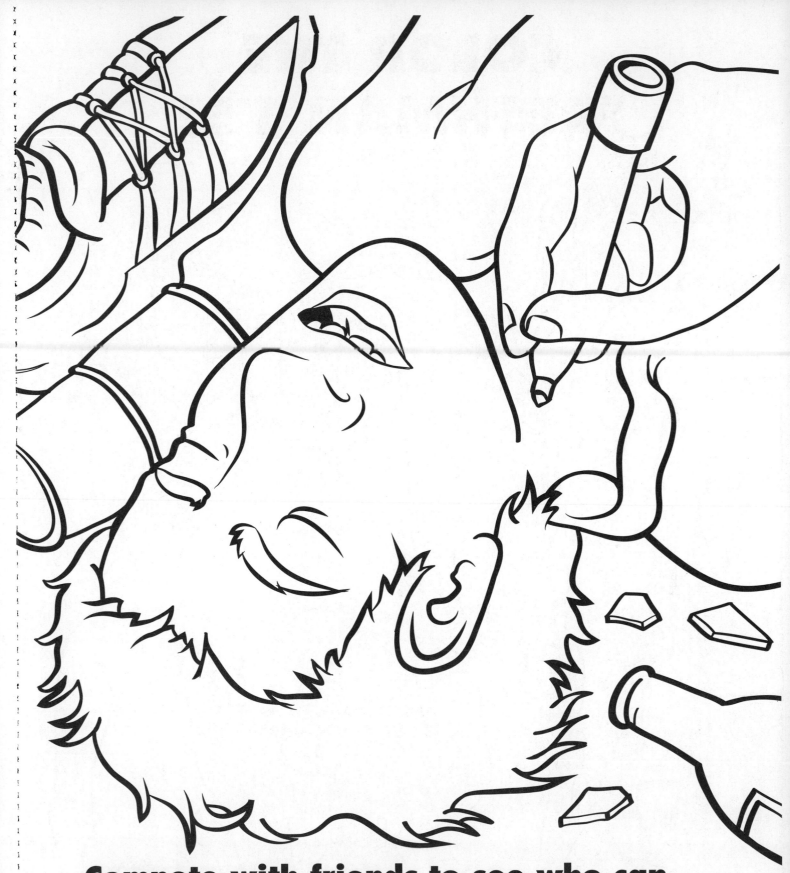

Compete with friends to see who can draw the most lifelike obscene image on this drunk guy's face!

COLOR THE FRESHMAN 15!

MUNCHIES MAN

RUSH WEEK RANGER

DELIVERY BOY

THANK YOU

HOMESICK COMMANDO

SNACK ATTACK

STRESSBALL

EXAM

DEPRESSIANA, THE EATER OF FEELINGS

POWER CHUG

PROFESSOR PIZZA

HANGOVERLORD

NIGHT CRAMMER

CULTURE SHOCK

INACTION JACKSON

CAPTAIN CARE PACKAGE

NETFLIX NAVIGATOR

CHIPS

The Freshman 15 are a superhero team sworn to help freshmen cope with the unfamiliar stresses of college life.

Collect them all!

YOUR PARENTS ARE VISITING!

Can you hurriedly locate the 6 things you forgot to hide before allowing them entrance into your living quarters?

(Solutions on page 55)

16

THE NICKNAME GAME

Match each on-campus personality with the nickname you and your friends remember them by.

"CHAZ"

"VIRGIN DAVE"

"MEATBALL SUB"

"AUNT MILDRED"

"BARACK PAJAMA"

"FAT CHAZ"

(Solutions on page 55)

DRAWING A BLANK

Use crayons or colored pencils to draw the dumb thing this college student was actually thinking about when he got called on in class.

BEFRIEND THE OLD GUY

He's 27! Unscramble the cool bands that only he knows about so he'll agree to buy you beer!

LARTUNE KILM THOLE

_____ ____ _____

COINS THUYO

____ _____

YM DLOBOY ENNALTIVE

__ _____ _____

LERATES-NINKEY

_____-_____

T. ERX

_._ ___

HET IPISEX

___ _____

YOJ SIVINIDO

___ _____

RASUNIDO RJ

_____ __

PEMEVTAN

_____

(Solutions on page 55)

COLLEGE DIVERSITY POSTER

This poster isn't diverse enough. Help your school simulate an atmosphere of inclusiveness by adding conjoined twins, amputees, and any other minorities you feel are underrepresented on your campus.

NAME THE COLLEGE BAND!

Write this band's new name on their drum kit by combining two or more original word choices from the list below!

The Lounge Presents

BLACK   **DEER**   **WOLF**   **CRYSTAL**

SKULL   **EXPLOSION**   **TEAM**

YOUTH   **MOTHER**   **DEATH**   **PARADE**

THE COOL R.A.

Rick is a cool R.A. Draw the off-limits behavior he's currently struggling to be cool about.

CONNECT THE DOTS

to help Jared figure out why he'll finish
college two years later than he planned.

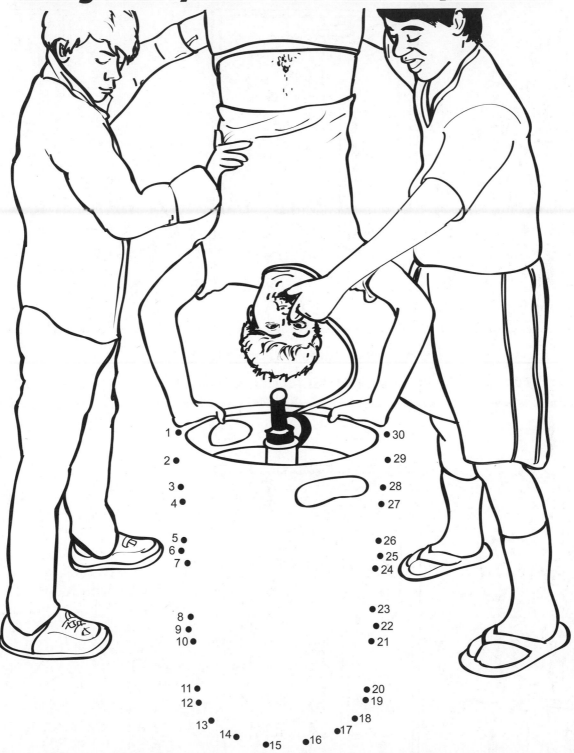

**(For added difficulty, complete this page while two
friends hoist you in the air for essentially no reason!)**

FIND THE DIFFERENCES!

Can you find 6 differences
between the image above and the one below?

(Solutions on page 55)

WALK OF SHAME MASK

Pretend to be someone who is actually proud of his or her decision-making when you walk home in this clever disguise.

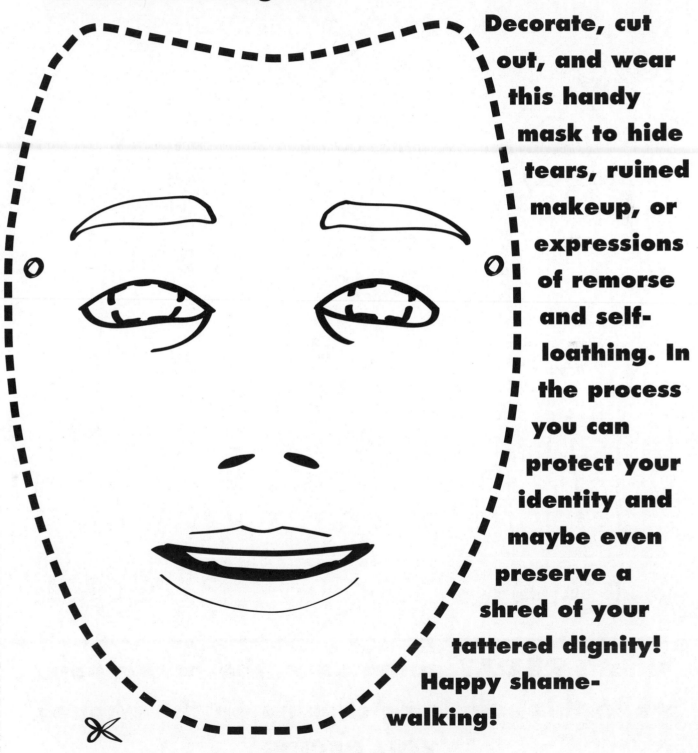

Decorate, cut out, and wear this handy mask to hide tears, ruined makeup, or expressions of remorse and self-loathing. In the process you can protect your identity and maybe even preserve a shred of your tattered dignity! Happy shame-walking!

LONG-DISTANCE RELATIONSHIP SECRETS

What's REALLY going on in the background
while this couple catches up on the phone?
YOU DECIDE.

CLASS PRESENTATION

You're about to present in front of the ENTIRE CLASS. Good thing you remembered the age-old trick of imagining everyone naked! Draw in your classmates' soothingly misshapen bodies.

Don't forget the hidden birthmarks, moles, and scars!

CREATE YOUR OWN COLLEGE PRANK!
Circle one word from each column to create your own wacky, hilarious goof!

VERB	OBJECT	PREPOSITION	NON SEQUITUR
PAINT	THE CAFETERIA	WITH	CHICKENS
STREAK	A NERD	AS	A GHOST
IMPERSONATE	THE QUAD	TO	BATMAN
PHOTOBOMB	YOUR ENTIRE CLASS	IN	HUMAN BLOOD
FLASH MOB	THE DEAN	AT	LIVE WEBCAM
PRANK CALL	THE RIVAL TEAM	FROM	A PTERODACTYL
BURN DOWN	CAMPUS SECURITY	IN FRONT OF	BARACK OBAMA
PEE ON	YOUR CRUSH	BEFORE	FARTS
EMBARRASS	SOMEONE'S PARENTS	DRESSED AS	THE ELDERLY
CROP DUST	YOURSELF	INSTEAD OF	A WHITE PERSON
POISON	AMERICA	ON	A FUNERAL
SEXT	PIZZA	INSIDE	MACAULAY CULKIN

PRANK NAME:

VISUAL AID:

Put this campus security guard in a situation way over his head!

BEER BONG EVERYTHING!

Color the journey each liquid will take before being guzzled by its recipient!

30

CONNECT THE DOTS
to help Ethan figure out why he'll never be invited to another party!

PRESSURE YOUR PEERS!

Simulate the college experience by matching each peer to his or her most susceptible form of social pressure!

(Solutions on page 57)

EMPTY NEST HOME MAKEOVER

What are your parents going to do with your empty room now that you're out of the house? Office? Exercise room? S&M dungeon? YOU DECIDE!

DROWNING IN DEBT

Research the financial commitments you've made in order to educate yourself, then draw in your future, postgraduate self!

$0

$5,000

$10,000

$15,000

$20,000

$25,000

$30,000

$40,000

$50,000

$60,000

$75,000

$100,000

$150,000

$200,000

WHAT ARE MY PRIORITIES?

This activity entails an ever-evolving, lifelong search to discover what is truly important to you, so be sure to place this page somewhere you can locate it at all times. The only word bank is the one inside your own fickle heart. Good luck!

```
W C A T S P G I N X I V J D U B L I S Y A S
Q F R I E N D S H I P I Z Z A F O K P V M E
O H T J X A H T D O G S N M O R V U R F Y J
M J F B U P M A C C E P T A N C E B I R D M
U O A R A S O T H P R O C R E A T I O N I U
S B M E L K N U A C A R S R B S P D R U G S
I S E L F R E S P E C T F I O H C S I V N C
C E G I R P Y D P V D S N A C K S H T A I H
L C T G E E H F I I N T E G R I T Y I G T I
F U N I E N E A N L S H O E S G B G Z I Y L
A R C O D I A M E D U C A T I O N I I N P L
S I A N O S L I S L E E P B A L H E N A O V
H T R A M G T L S T I N R E A D I N G K R I
I Y E L T P H Y S I C A L F I T N E S S N B
O N E I V F O O D M Y B R O S J K B O O Z E
N C R E A T I V E E X P R E S S I O N H N S
```

BONUS ACTIVITY: There are 50 different priorities hidden inside this puzzle. Spend time finding them all to teach yourself about the dangers of having bad priorities!

Can you find and color all 60 red Solo cups at this keg party?

CRAM YOUR HEAD WITH USELESS INFORMATION!

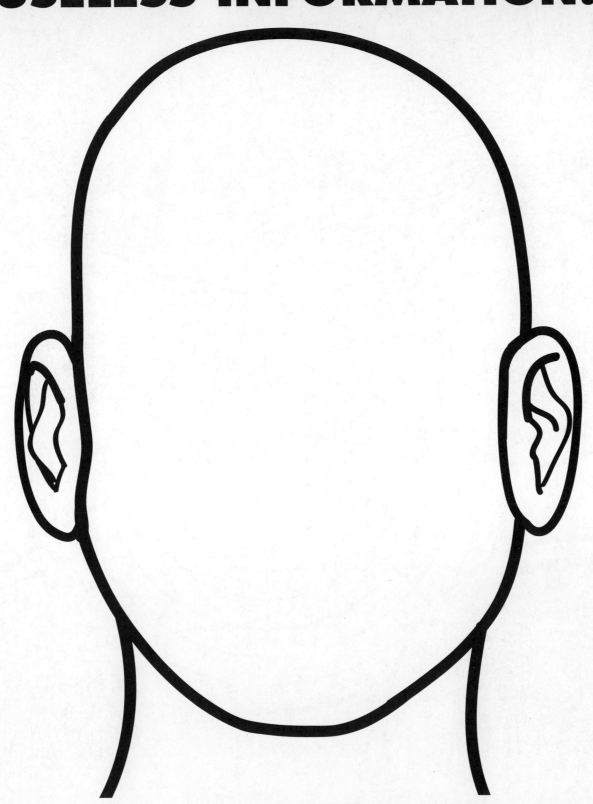

SO ALL YOUR FRIENDS DECIDED TO STUDY ABROAD...

Pretend you were there too by drawing yourself into each of these life-changing, overseas moments!

FRANCE

ITALY

AUSTRALIA

NORTH KOREA

CONNECT THE DOTS
to help Tanya figure out the meaning of life.

(Solutions on page 57)

MAKE A STUDENT FILM

PRETENTIOUS, ONE-WORD TITLE: _____

REASON MAIN CHARACTER IS SAD: _____

LOVE INTEREST (circle one):

Prostitute   Unattainably hot girl   Dying prostitute

ANTAGONIST (circle one):

Rich guy   The devil   Society

STORYBOARD YOUR MAGNUM OPUS BELOW:

1	**2**
ESTABLISHING SHOT OF:	**PUSH IN ON:**
3	**4**
WHIP PAN TO:	**FADE TO BLACK AS:**

DEFENSE OF WHY ENTIRE FILM WAS IN BLACK-AND-WHITE:

_____

_____

DEGREES OF SUCCESS

Match your degree of choice to the job it will actually land you in the real world!

COMMUNICATIONS

PHILOSOPHY

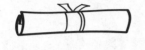

POLITICAL SCIENCE

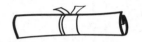

ART HISTORY

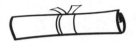

JOURNALISM

SUBSTITUTE TEACHER

SANDWICH ARTIST

PRODUCTION ASSISTANT

STREET PERFORMER

FREELANCE VIDEO BLOGGER

(Solutions on page 57)

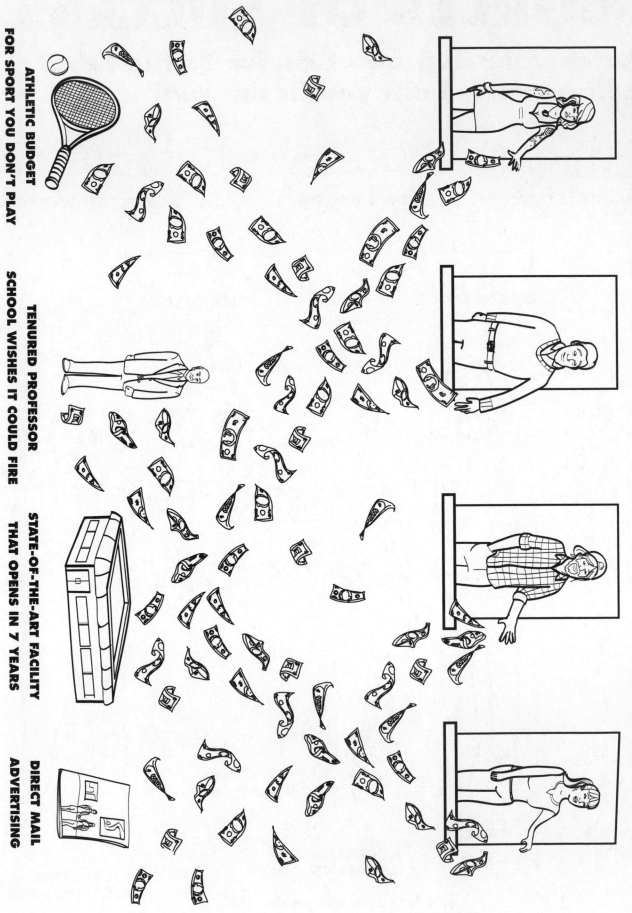

DESIGN YOUR OWN SADISTIC, VAGUELY HOMOEROTIC HAZING RITUAL!

SCHOOL COLORS

What powerful message from the fans inspired the game-winning touchdown?

Spell it out in team colors on the flabby torsos of your choosing!

CONNECT THE DOTS

to help Eric realize the mushrooms he ate had magic powers.

Then finish drawing his mystical vision quest!

WHO DOESN'T BELONG?

Color the students who belong in this picture while cruelly excluding the others!

CYNICISM ACTIVITY FUN PAGE

College has taught you to question and criticize all of your deepest held beliefs. Prove how cynical you REALLY are by saying something snarky about each of the following universally well-liked subjects:

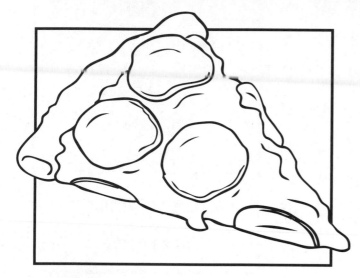

PIZZA _____

_____

MUSIC _____

_____

PUPPIES _____

_____

TOM HANKS _____

_____

WORD SEARCH
FOR EMPLOYMENT IN AN UNFRIENDLY JOB MARKET!

Words to search for:

R V G P X E B I M G T Z O Z
E I C O W R O X E E B T D L
L B A P L S P B D B L N J Y
T Y O Q D O P A N I C O H R
I R E O E N O S C N H K C A
G A N W P A R E N T S E B U
I U P C R B T M L E D L X M
O M F J E K U E J R G I Z A
N A R T S G N N E N B V E Y
C Y C B S O I T A S H E S B
O B A R I S T A L H R L I O
N D R J O B Y P H I R I N G
F O E W N R F T S P E H T T
L Z E K Q I T N K E U O E I
I T R U L E A T E D I O R M
T I F N R S O R L E P D V I
S M U E N C N W F B V R I L
C F D R O W R F U T U R E F
O J M S F P G W S D O I W V

JOB
INTERVIEW
CAREER
HIRING
OPPORTUNITY
LIVELIHOOD
FUTURE

Words to avoid:

PARENTS
BASEMENT
DEBT
PANIC
DEPRESSION
INTERNSHIP
BARISTA

(Solutions on page 57)

POSTPONE YOUR LIFE!
How long can YOU avoid reality?

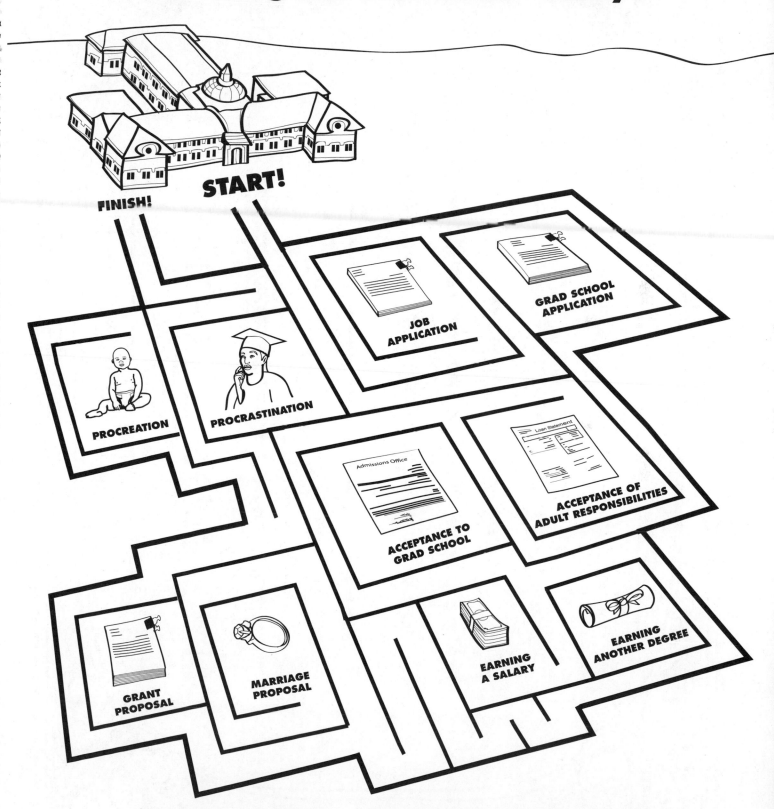

FINISH!

START!

JOB APPLICATION

GRAD SCHOOL APPLICATION

PROCREATION

PROCRASTINATION

ACCEPTANCE TO GRAD SCHOOL

ACCEPTANCE OF ADULT RESPONSIBILITIES

GRANT PROPOSAL

MARRIAGE PROPOSAL

EARNING A SALARY

EARNING ANOTHER DEGREE

GRAD SCHOOL ACTIVITY FUN PAGE

THE ADULTHOOD INSTITUTE

ADULTHOOD CERTIFICATE

This document is to certify that

_____

(ADULT'S NAME)

*has successfully sublimated his or her
childlike need for parental love into a raging
addiction and has therefore
completed the transition into adulthood.*

ISSUER'S SIGNATURE

DATE

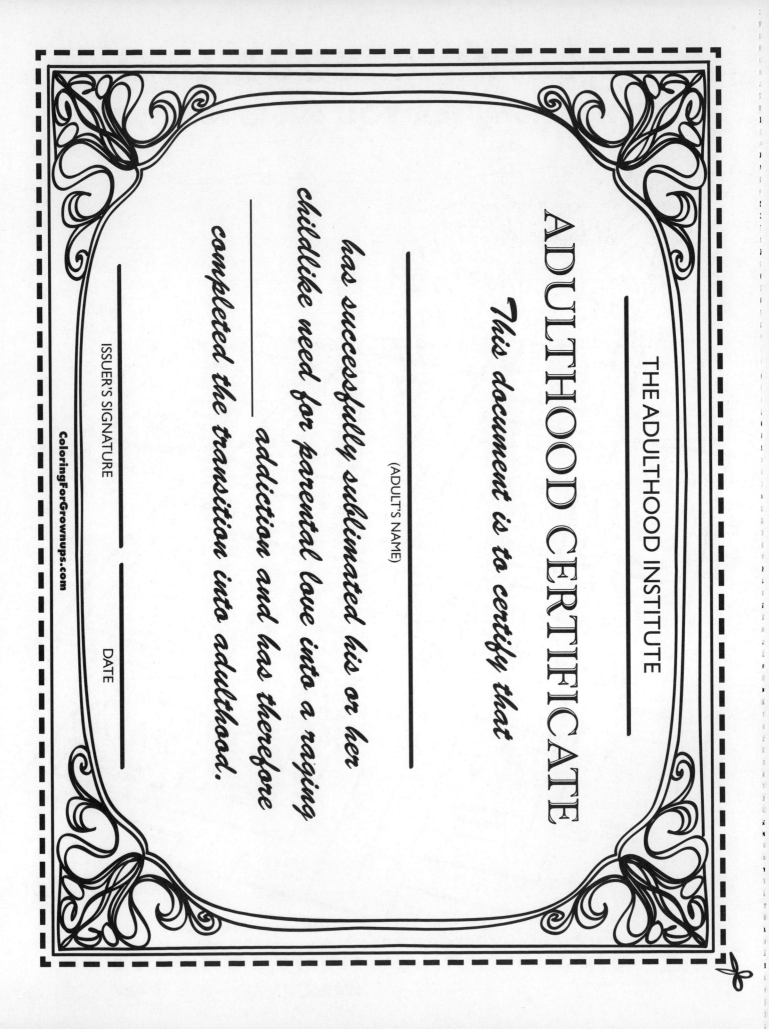

ColoringForGrownups.com

REALISTIC EMERGENCY CONTACT SHEET

NAME: _____ BIRTHDATE: _____

ALLERGIES: _____

WHICH PRESCRIPTION DRUGS I TAKE: _____

WHICH NONPRESCRIPTION/RECREATIONAL DRUGS I TAKE: _____

_____

_____

POTENTIALLY SOBER FRIENDS TO CALL WHEN EVERY RIDE HAS LEFT ME:

_____   _____

_____   _____

PREFERRED LOCATION(S) FOR THE DISPOSAL OF MY UNCONSCIOUS BODY:

_____

_____

PSYCHO FRIENDS TO CALL IN CASE I END UP IN A FIGHT:

_____   _____

_____   _____

DRUNK DIAL DO NOT CALL LIST

NAME	#	REASON	SEVERITY (1-5 FROWNY FACES)

PLEASE SLAP ME IN THE FACE WHEN: _____

**CUT OUT THIS PAGE AND KEEP IT ON YOUR PERSON AT ALL TIMES
FOR A MARGINALLY LESS REGRET-FILLED COLLEGE EXPERIENCE!**

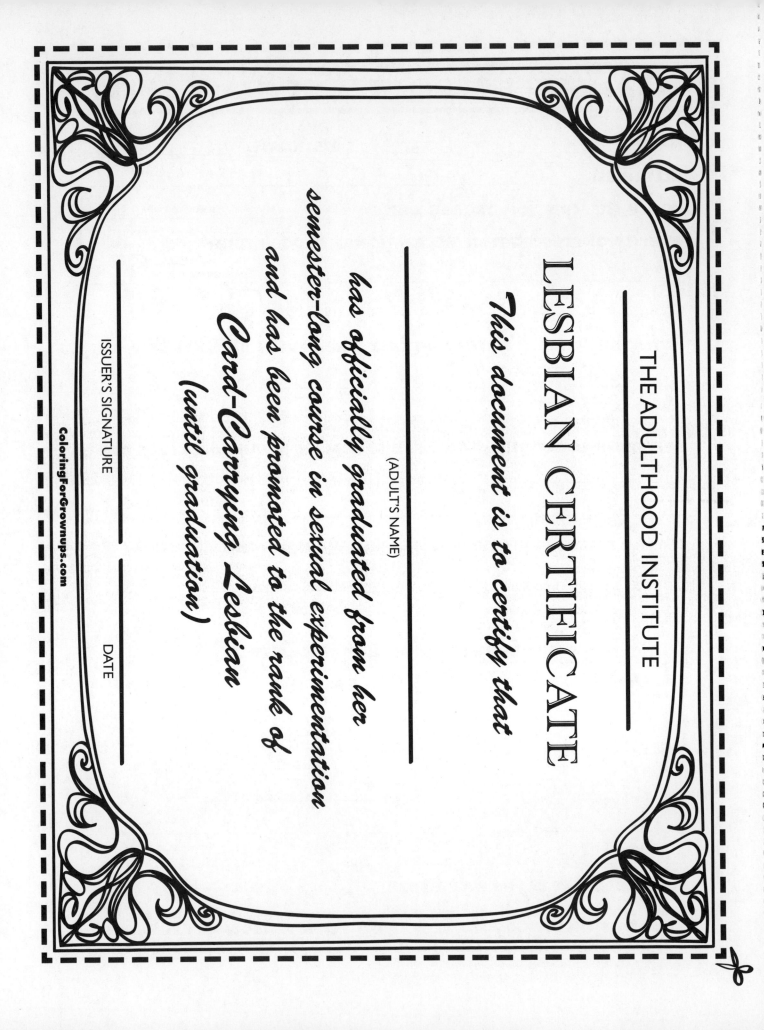

THE ADULTHOOD INSTITUTE

LESBIAN CERTIFICATE

This document is to certify that

_____

(ADULT'S NAME)

has officially graduated from her semester-long course in sexual experimentation and has been promoted to the rank of

Card-Carrying Lesbian

(until graduation)

_____
ISSUER'S SIGNATURE

_____
DATE

SOLUTIONS

YOUR PARENTS ARE VISITING!

Can you hurriedly locate the 6 things you forgot to hide before allowing them entrance into your living quarters?

P. 16

1. Your mom hates her new haircut and will intentionally ruin the entire day if she looks in this mirror.
2. President Thomas Jefferson invented the very first swivel chair. Your parents hate Thomas Jefferson!
3. Mom and Dad didn't home-school you for 13 years just to have you get to college and start reading books.
4. Analog clocks remind your parents of books. Get rid of it.
5. This trophy always reminds your dad how much he likes kicking things. LOOK OUT!
6. If your parents see you displaying this photo of the family they abducted you from as a child, things are going to get SUPER awkward. Don't say we didn't warn you!

FIND THE DIFFERENCES!

Can you find 6 differences between the image above and the one below?

P. 24

CONGRATULATIONS! You victoriously located all six differences (and one slightly heinous double standard)!

THE NICKNAME GAME

Match each on-campus personality with the nickname you and your friends remember them by.

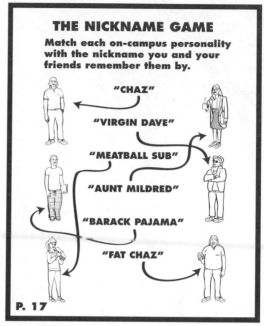

"CHAZ"

"VIRGIN DAVE"

"MEATBALL SUB"

"AUNT MILDRED"

"BARACK PAJAMA"

"FAT CHAZ"

P. 17

YOU DID IT! You successfully reduced six human beings to a collection of pithy, derisive aliases, thereby saving yourself the trouble of ever having to get to know them personally!

BEFRIEND THE OLD GUY

He's 27! Unscramble the cool bands that only he knows about so he'll agree to buy you beer!

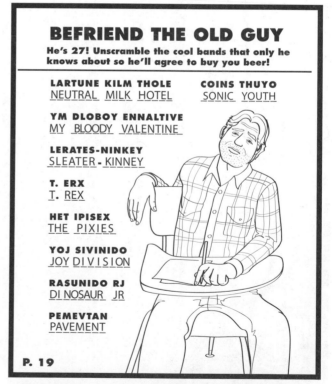

LARTUNE KILM THOLE
NEUTRAL MILK HOTEL

COINS THUYO
SONIC YOUTH

YM DLOBOY ENNALTIVE
MY BLOODY VALENTINE

LERATES-NINKEY
SLEATER-KINNEY

T. ERX
T. REX

HET IPISEX
THE PIXIES

YOJ SIVINIDO
JOY DIVISION

RASUNIDO RJ
DINOSAUR JR

PEMEVTAN
PAVEMENT

P. 19

Because he saw you looking in the back of the book for help, the old guy has decided he's too busy to buy you beer today. But he guesses you can take an after-class drag off his one-hitter in exchange for the Stats homework, if you're down.

THE ADULTHOOD INSTITUTE

SLACKER DIPLOMA

This document is to certify that

_____

(ADULT'S NAME)

has demonstrated advanced proficiency in couch-sitting, Internet-video-watching, haul-packing, and blunt-rolling and has been granted authorization to complete college and enter the unemployed workforce.

_____
ISSUER'S SIGNATURE

_____
DATE

SOLUTIONS

PRESSURE YOUR PEERS!

Simulate the college experience by matching each peer to his or her most susceptible form of social pressure!

P. 32

1. Tabitha promised her parents she wouldn't drink beer before turning 21. Try peer pressuring her into watching some Internet porn, thereby making her depressed about humanity and ready to numb her feelings. Peer pressure accomplished!

2. Ronald told himself he wouldn't let anyone peer pressure him into rollerblading ever again. Pressure him to get stoned with you, then peer pressure him to put on the rollerblades while his defenses are lowered. Peer pressure: 1, Ronald: 0.

3. Carmen has never smoked a cigarette, but theoretically might be receptive to the idea after a round of safe and consensual coitus. Score one for Big Tobacco (and peer pressure).

4. Kevin hates Satanism but LOVES pizza. Peer pressure him in to attending a Satanist pizza party and let pizza (and Satan) do the rest. Then simply sit back, collect your peer pressure commission check, and rejoice in the corruption of yet another peer!

DEGREES OF SUCCESS

Match your degree of choice to the job it will actually land you in the real world!

P. 43

You completed the puzzle and achieved success! In this coloring book, at least.

CONNECT THE DOTS

to help Tanya figure out the meaning of life.

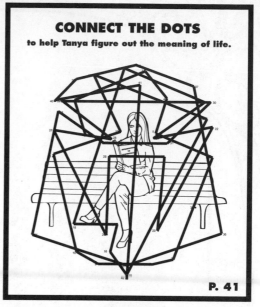

P. 41

SOLUTION:
Just like the image above, life has no inherent meaning. It is the onus of the individual to give meaning to life and to live it authentically.

You have now completed Existentialism 101.

P. 50

WORD SEARCH

FOR EMPLOYMENT IN AN UNFRIENDLY JOB MARKET!

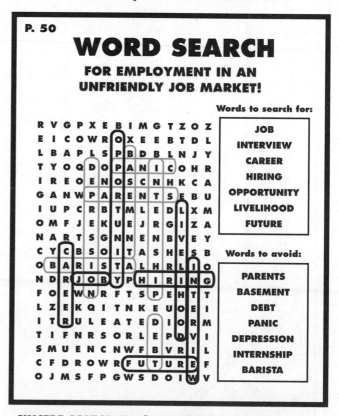

Words to search for:

| JOB |
| INTERVIEW |
| CAREER |
| HIRING |
| OPPORTUNITY |
| LIVELIHOOD |
| FUTURE |

Words to avoid:

| PARENTS |
| BASEMENT |
| DEBT |
| PANIC |
| DEPRESSION |
| INTERNSHIP |
| BARISTA |

SINCERE ADVICE: Work very hard and be nice to people and good things will happen to you no matter what field you enter!

MORE IMPORTANTLY: Don't leave us any Amazon reviews saying our book had a purely cynical outlook on the job market, because you will make yourself look like a big, dirty liar!

THE ADULTHOOD INSTITUTE

ROOMMATE DIPLOMA

This document is to certify that

_____

(ROOMMATE'S NAME)

has officially graduated from being that weirdo I used to complain about around my friends to being someone I actually, kind of, almost like. Congratulations.

_____
ISSUER'S SIGNATURE

_____
DATE

Credits

WRITTEN AND ILLUSTRATED BY
Ryan Hunter and Taige Jensen

ADDITIONAL ILLUSTRATIONS BY

Mike Force
Chloe Harrison-Ach
Avery Monsen
Nic Rad

Chris Silva
Kevin Wheatley
Justin Winslow
Byerly Young

CREATIVE TEAM

Aleks Arcabascio
Zach Broussard
Alene Latimer
Jenn Lyon

James McCarthy
Avery Monsen
Quinn Scott
Achilles Stamatelaky

Acknowledgments

Everyone listed above rescued us from oblivion in one way or another. We also owe a massive debt of thanks to all of the wonderful people who worked on this book from Penguin and Plume, many of whom we will probably never meet, thanks to the miracle of the Internet. Our editor Becky Cole deserves our most passionate and sincere gratitude, immediately followed by several thousand apologies. Thanks also to Jason Allen Ashlock and Meredith Dawson, without whom our lives would be thoroughly bookless.

For the third consecutive time we have no other choice than to specifically call out Jenn Lyon for consistently being the glue that keeps this whole thing together. We'd also like to give special thanks to Dylan Angell, Aleks Arcabascio, Milena Brown, Tyler Jackson, Kate Napolitano, Lauren Reeves, and Gail Werner, as well as every teacher who ever encouraged us to follow our dreams, without knowing it would one day lead to the volume of barf and wiener jokes you now hold in your hands.

Collegiately,
Ryan & Taige

About the Authors

Ryan Hunter and Taige Jensen are a New York–based pair of writer-actor-filmmaker-author-illustrators. Only one of them attended college, yet they are both rich and famous coloring book impresarios, so take that for whatever it's worth.

In addition to making three books together, their sketch comedy channel POYKPAC has garnered over 79 million views on YouTube. Follow them around the Internet:

TWITTER:	@ryan_hunter	@taige	@colorfulhumor
WEBSITE/TUMBLR:		ColoringForGrownups.com	
FACEBOOK:		facebook.com/ColoringForGrownups	
INSTAGRAM:	coloringforgrownups	YOUTUBE:	POYKPAC

AUTHOR ILLUSTRATIONS BY CHRIS SILVA